Kimono
きもの
日本語 Level 1
Workbook

by
Sue Burnham
and
Yukiko Saegusa

Illustrated by
Bettina Guthridge
Edited by
Helen McBride
Designed by
Josie Semmler

CIS Educational

First published 1990 by CIS Educational

Reprinted 1996 by CIS•Heinemann
a division of Reed International Books Australia Pty Ltd
22 Salmon Street, Port Melbourne, Victoria 3207
Telephone (03) 9245 7111
Facsimile (03) 9245 7333
World Wide Web http://www.hi.com.au
Email info@hi.com.au

Offices in Sydney, Brisbane, Adelaide and Perth.
Associated companies, branches and representatives around the world.

2006	2005	2004	2003	2002	2001	2000	
23	22	21	20	19	18	17	16

Edited by Helen McBride
Designed and typeset by Josie Semmler on Apple Macintosh
Illustrated by Bettina Guthridge
Additional illustrations by Bill Farr
Crane character by Randy Glusac

Printed by Craft Print Pte Ltd

ISBN 0 949919 67 5

Contents ・ もくじ

Introduction ・ はじめに

The *Kimono Workbook* contains a wide variety of exercises and activities based on the language and cultural information presented in the corresponding units of the *Kimono* textbook.

The Japanese script

Hiragana is presented in two intensive units, ひらがな 一 and 二, which come after units 2 and 4. Both the *Kimono* text and *Workbook* have been designed so that students can complete units 1 and 2 without having been formally introduced to the *hiragana* script. However because of the large amount of writing practice required, particularly in ひらがな 一, it is suggested that you start introducing *hiragana* from the outset and have students gradually work through the ひらがな一 unit while doing units 1 and 2. In any case, students should have completed ひらがな一 before they start unit 3. They are then ready to start ひらがな二, which they complete while doing units 3 and 4.

Thus, in units 1 and 2 students are only expected to recognise *hiragana* and *kanji* numbers, they do not need to reproduce them. In units 3 and 4 reproduction in limited to the *hiragana* taught in ひらがな 一.

Each unit in the *Workbook* comprises the following elements:

ききましょう

This section contains listening comprehension exercises for each unit. These exercises are performed on the *Kimono* cassettes.

れんしゅう しましょう

These exercises and activities account for the bulk of the material in the *Workbook*. They provide written reinforcement of the language treated orally in each unit and come in a variety of forms. In addition, each unit includes a puzzle and a reading comprehension exercise related to the cartoon story.

日本に ついて

Under this heading are exercises and activities which enhance and, in some cases, extend the cultural material presented in most units of the *Kimono* textbook.

ひらがな 一

In ひらがな 一, the *hiragana* symbols are introduced by sound line. For each symbol there is a model, partly screened examples displaying stroke order and two examples for tracing over. Three sizes of blocks of empty squares are provided for practice.

For each sound line there is a section entitled かきましょう in which students practise writing the symbols they have just learned to complete words which are associated to pictures.

In addition to the かきましょう sections, after the が, だ, ぱ and わ sound lines there is a れんしゅう しましょう section which recycles all *hiragana* symbols learned so far. In the exercises in this section the emphasis is on recognition and reproduction of these *hiragana* only using words and pictures that students have seen.

ひらがな 二

In the ひらがな 二 section, students practise writing the *kanji* numbers as well as combination sounds, little つ and words with long vowel sounds. Practice squares for writing both horizontally and vertically are provided.

For each of the four sections there are れんしゅう しましょう exercises to provide further reinforcement.

In both of the *hiragana* units students are exposed to a lot more vocabulary than used in the *Kimono* textbook. However, it is restricted to these units, always associated with a picture and students are only expected to reproduce it in written form. In most cases the vocabulary used is associated with specific themes, such as parts of the body, seasons etc., or culturally based.

ききましょう

A Hose くん like you, is practising greeting and farewelling his friends in Japanese. Put a tick in the grid showing what he said to each person.

	good morning	morning!	good evening	goodbye	see you later
Amanda さん					
ゆうこさん					
せんせい					
はなこさん					
Terii くん					
みなさん					

B You will hear some people greeting or farewelling each other. Write the number under the picture indicating the greeting you heard.

C Here are the numbers 1 - 6 written in *kanji*.
In each row highlight the two numbers you hear.

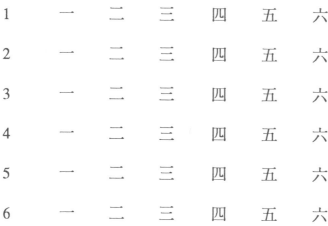

1	一	二	三	四	五	六
2	一	二	三	四	五	六
3	一	二	三	四	五	六
4	一	二	三	四	五	六
5	一	二	三	四	五	六
6	一	二	三	四	五	六

D Are you hearing someone being surprised, apologising, giving
a greeting or saying goodbye?
Use your highlighter pen to show that you have understood.

1	surprise	apology	greeting	farewell
2	surprise	apology	greeting	farewell
3	surprise	apology	greeting	farewell
4	surprise	apology	greeting	farewell
5	surprise	apology	greeting	farewell

れんしゅう しましょう

A All of the きもの characters are helping you to count in Japanese. Can you draw a line connecting each character with the *kanji* for the number they are indicating. One has already been done for you.

四　二　五　一　三　六

B From the alternatives given below each picture, highlight which expression is being used.

じゃ またね。

Hose です。

1　a　おなまえは?
　　b　すみません。

2　a　さようなら。
　　b　こんにちは。

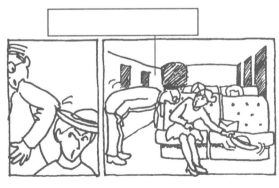

3　a　おはよう。
　　b　おはよう ございます。

4　a　すみません。
　　b　さようなら。

C Terii くん has done some of his maths homework in *kanji* numbers. Can you correct it?

1 一 + 二 = 三

2 四 ÷ 二 = 二

3 六 ÷ 三 = 四

4 二 x 三 = 六

5 四 + 一 = 六

6 三 − 二 = 一

7 六 − 五 = 二

What mark did he get? _____

D See if you can find the following *hiragana* words in the cartoon story. How many times does each word appear?

1 せんせい   (teacher)   _____

2 こんにちは   (hello/hi)   _____

3 さようなら   (goodbye)   _____

E Each of the words below has one *hiragana* missing. Decide which of the following *hiragana* is needed to complete each word, and draw a line connecting them. Highlight the word that is not a greeting.

| は | う | み | ま | ん |

3 じゃ …たね

5 お…よう

1 さよ…なら

4 こ…にちは

2 す…ません

F The Japanese teacher, ほんだ せんせい has written these new words on the board. Terii くん has copied them into his book, but in a different order. Check that he has copied them all by drawing a line between the same words in each list.

1 こんにちは   1 おはよう
2 さようなら   2 こんばんは
3 すみません   3 すみません
4 おはよう   4 こんにちは
5 おやすみ なさい   5 おはよう ございます
6 こんばんは   6 じゃ またね
7 おはよう ございます   7 さようなら
8 じゃ またね   8 おやすみ なさい

G Someone has already done this crossword - try to work out some clues in English for it.

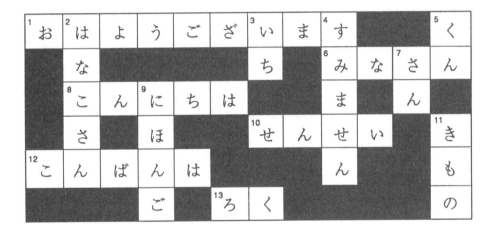

たて   よこ

2 _____   1 _____

3 _____   6 _____

4 _____   8 _____

5 _____   10 _____

7 _____   12 _____

9 _____   13 _____

11 _____

日本に ついて

一 Some Japanese words have become well known in English because of the products they represent. What products do you associate with these names?

1 Toyota _____   6 Shiseido _____

2 Noritake _____   7 Seiko _____

3 Honda _____   8 Ryobi _____

4 Yamaha _____   9 Fuji _____

5 Akai _____   10 Fujitsu _____

二 Match the articles on the left-hand side with the name of the Japanese company on the right-hand side.

1 cars   1 NEC

2 cameras   2 Mazda

3 computers   3 Sony

4 walkmans/radios   4 Canon

5 watches   5 Sharp

6 televisions/videos   6 Citizen

三 Make a list of at least ten things that you use either at home or at school that are 'made in Japan'. Compare your list with a friend.

_____   _____

_____   _____

_____   _____

_____   _____

_____   _____

四 Find out what each of the following traditional Japanese activities are.

1 origami

_____

2 ikebana

_____

3 bonsai

_____

ききましょう

A はなこさん is helping Hose くん study for a test. She is holding up
lots of different objects and asking him what they are in 日本語.
Show that you understand by marking the objects as you hear
Hose くん say them.

B Listen to the following mini conversations and decide whether the
statements given here are correct. Mark each box with a tick or a cross.

1 ☐ Someone asked ゆうこさん her name.

2 ☐ Someone was given a ruler.

3 ☐ Amanda is the number 2 player.

4 ☐ Someone asked よしおくん his age.

5 ☐ Theo introduced himself.

C The Japanese teacher is showing a Japanese visitor around the school. She sees a group of students who are studying Japanese. She introduces the visitor and then asks the students to introduce themselves in Japanese of course!

Place a tick next to the names of the students who were there.

	present	age
Peter		
Ken		
Helen		
Anne		
Mario		
John		
Sue		

The visitor is most impressed. She asks their ages. Write down the age of each student.

D Understanding numbers is an important skill for 'getting by' in Japan, even for those who have only learned a little Japanese. Imagine that you are in a city in Japan and have asked for different bits of important information. All you really need to understand in the answer is the number, so concentrate on listening for that and write it down when you hear it. You don't need to use *kanji* numbers here, just write the figure.

1 The number of the bus going to the station. _____

2 The final score of the baseball match between the *Giants* and *Seibu* that you were watching on T.V. last night.

   Giants _____   Seibu _____

3 The number of the platform for the しんかんせん. _____

4 The time the department store opens. _____

5 The time the department store shuts. _____

6 The number of your friend すずきさん who is running in a local marathon. _____

れんしゅうしましょう

A Draw a line to match each question or statement to a suitable answer.

1 おなまえは?　　　　　　　　1 はい、えんぴつ です。

2 なんさい ですか。　　　　　　2 Amanda です。

3 日本語で なん ですか。　　　3 十二さい です。

4 Purezento です。どうぞ。　　4 けしgomu です。

5 これは えんぴつ ですか。　　5 ありがとう。

B Highlight the odd word out.

1 Which of these won't you find in your pencil-case?

えんぴつ　　　　　pen　　　　　けしgomu　　　　　ほん

2 Which of these can't you open?

ほん　　　　　doa　　　　　こくばん　　　　　まど

3 Which of these can't you close?

ものさし　　　　　ふでばこ　　　　　まど　　　　　doa

4 Which of these is not an even number?

八　　　　　十　　　　　十三　　　　　四

5 Which of these *kanji* numbers can be read in two ways?

七　　　　　六　　　　　五　　　　　八

6 Which of these is not a question?

おなまえは?　　　なんさい ですか。　　　どうぞ よろしく。　　　なん ですか。

C You are labelling in 日本語 some of your things and some other things in the classroom. Where will you put these labels?

1 こくばん＿＿＿＿＿＿＿　　　5 えんぴつ ＿＿＿＿＿＿＿

2 まど ＿＿＿＿＿＿＿　　　6 ほん ＿＿＿＿＿＿＿

3 doa ＿＿＿＿＿＿＿　　　7 ものさし ＿＿＿＿＿＿＿

4 ふでばこ＿＿＿＿＿＿＿

D The きもの characters are having a sports challenge. You are to be the commentator - match the statements below with each picture. In the box next to each character, write the number of the statement.

1 十三ばんは ほんだせんせい です。
2 十二ばんは Terii くん です。
3 七ばんは ゆうこさん です。
4 九ばんは はなこさん です。
5 十一ばんは Hose くん です。
6 八ばんは Amanda さん です。

E まんが
Look at the まんが on pages 十三 and 十四 in your textbook, and answer the following.

1 What time of the day is it?

☐ morning   ☐ afternoon   ☐ evening

2 What joke do the twins play on Hose くん?

_____

_____

3 The twins and Amanda さん hand Hose くん lots of items he has dropped. Highlight which items they give him.

けしgomu   えんぴつ   ものさし   ふでばこ   ほん

4 What is Amanda さん referring to when she asks,
これは なん ですか。

_____

F Find the classroom objects listed in the word maze and highlight them. They are written both vertically and horizontally. Four *hiragana* will remain to spell out another very important classroom 'item'!

ものさし
こくばん
ほん
えんぴつ
まど
ふでばこ

も	ほ	ん	こ	え
の	せ	ん	く	ん
さ	ま		ば	ぴ
し	ど	せ	ん	つ
ふ	で	ば	こ	い

mystery word: _____

G これは なん ですか。

Using the *kanji* numbers join the dots using the number chain below.

5 ~ 7 ~ 13 ~ 9 ~ 1 ~ 12 ~ 4 ~ 8 ~ 10 ~ 2 ~ 11 ~ 3 ~ 6 ~ 13 ~
3 ~ 7 ~ 11 ~ 1 ~ 5 ~ 12 ~ 8 ~ 4 ~ 9 ~ 1 ~ 6 ~ 2 ~ 3 ~ 7 ~ 12 ~ 9

Start here 五

日本に ついて

Japanese writing

Look at this article about a cake shop in Tokyo, and complete the exercises on the opposite page. Refer to page 十一 of your textbook for the explanations on Japanese writing.

おいしいケーキ屋さん

行動力のあるOLは、おいしい店の噂を
聞けばどこへでも出かけていきます。
だから職場から離れても、ほんとうに
おいしい店はちゃんと知っているのです。
どこのOLにも人気のある店やその地
いろいろ楽しい話題を持っているケーキ屋
さんをご紹介しましょう。

ホームケーキ

ここへ来ればお菓子を作る材料と道具が全
部揃います。経営者の小林潤子さんが、か
ってお菓子の材料が思うように揃わず不自
由したのが開店のきっかけでした。また、
ホームケーキ主催で、有名なお菓子屋さん
のチーフを先生とする講習会が定期的に開
かれるので、技術の習得もできます。デコ
レーションの方法など基本的なこともカー
ド式でわかりやすく教えてもらえます。

東京都目黒区自由ヶ丘一一七ー5ー3 ☎03
(724)0039 (営)10時30分 18時30分
(休)第二、第四水曜日

一 With three different coloured highlighter pens, mark on the heading the words written in

  · kanji   · hiragana   · katakana

二 Mark which writing is in よこがき (horizontal) and which is in たてがき (vertical).

三 On the よこがき highlight five *kanji*.

四 On the たてがき highlight three *katakana*.

五 Highlight five *hiragana* that you recognise.

日本に いきましょう!   Let's go to Japan!

一 How long will it take to fly to Japan?

_____

二 How much will the trip cost?

_____

三 You want to ring your friend in Japan to say when you are arriving. You want to ring at 8.00 p.m. Japanese time. At what time must you call?

_____

四 Your airline offers you a deal, which allows you to visit five cities in Japan. Which cities do you choose? Refer to the map of Japan on page 7 of your textbook.

  1 _____

  2 _____

  3 _____

  4 _____

  5 _____

あ	あ	あ	あ		
あ	あ				
い	い	い			
い	い				
う	う	う			
う	う				
え	え	え			
え	え				
お	お	お	お		
お	お				

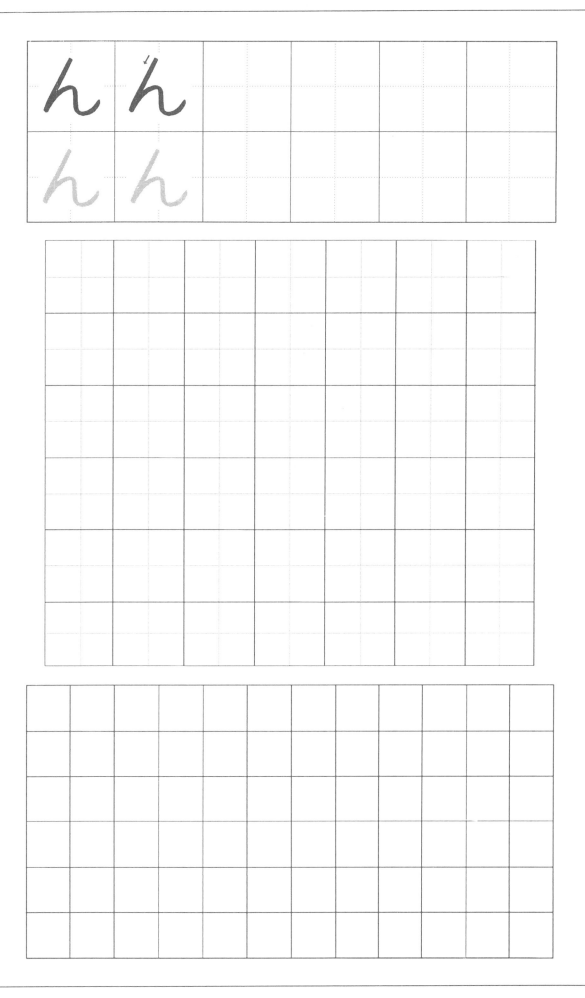

かきましょう

Complete the words using the symbol at the beginning of the line.

あ

	た	ま

	ひ	る

	き

い

	ぬ

	ち

	す

	た	だ	き	ま	す

う

	ま

	ち

	さ	ぎ

	し

え

□ ん ぴ つ

□ い が

□ い ご

□ き

お

□ な か

□ り が み

□ か し

□ ん が く

ん

は な こ さ □

せ □ せ い

と し お く □

す み ま せ □

かかかか
かか
きききき
きき
くく
くく
けけけけ
けけ
ここここ
ここ

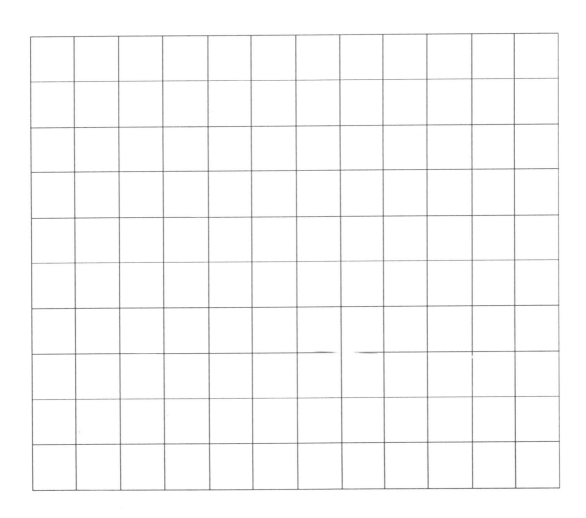

かきましょう

Complete the words using the symbol at the beginning of the line.

か

	え	る

	お

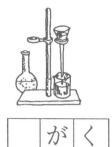

	が	く

	ら	て

き

	も	の

	た	な	い

	い	て

く

	る	ま

	ち

	じ

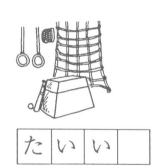

た	い	い	

け

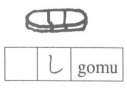

	し	gomu

	ん	じ	く	ん

	い	こ	さ	ん

	い	い	ち	く	ん

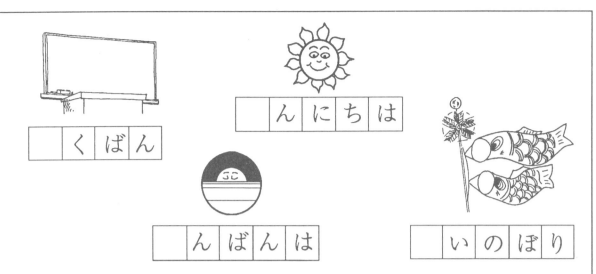

こ

	く	ば	ん

	ん	に	ち	は

	ん	ば	ん	は

	い	の	ぼ	り

If you add ゛ to the symbols in the K line sounds, you make G sounds.
In the first set of boxes, complete the word by using the symbol at the
beginning of the line. Then rewrite the word in the second set of boxes.
Any symbols that you haven't learned yet have been done for you.

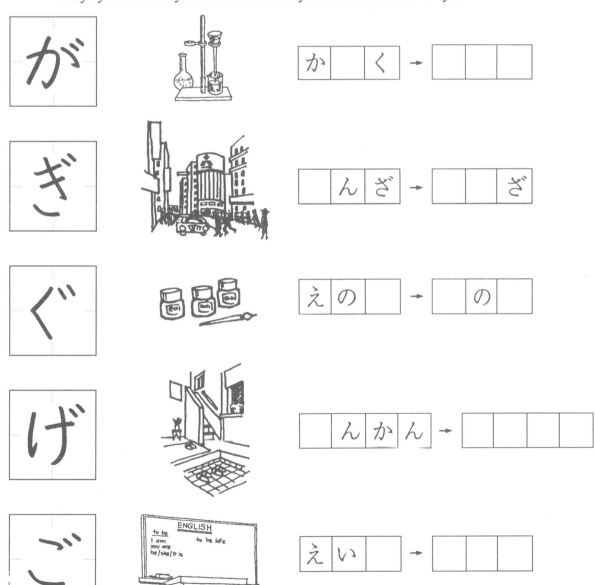

が

ぎ

ぐ

げ

ご

か		く	→		

	ん	ざ	→			ざ

え	の		→		の	

	ん	か	ん	→				

え	い		→			

ひらがな一 ● 二十一

れんしゅう しましょう

A These animals all have the same first sound. Complete each word.

| | ま | | さ | ぎ | | し |

B Complete these names for school subjects.

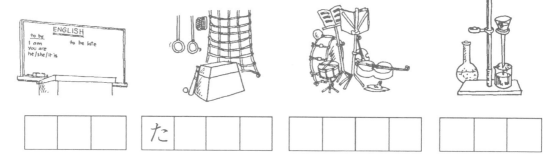

| | | | | た | | | | | | | | | | | |

C Write these Japanese words for different places in ひらがな.

| | | | | | | | ち | | | | ざ |

D Read these words aloud to a partner.

1 あき
2 えき
3 いいえ
4 えいが
5 かがく
6 えいご
7 かお
8 ええ
9 おんがく

E Draw a line to match these words with the pictures.

かお

no

おりがみ

あき

いいえ

ええ

けいこさん

yes

F You are now able to write three lines of the ひらがな chart.
Fill in this blank chart with as many ひらがな as you can.

	A	I	U	E	O
K					
G					

(n)	

さ　さ　さ　さ

さ　さ

し　し

し　し

す　す　ず

す　す

せ　せ　せ　せ

せ　せ

そ　そ

そ　そ

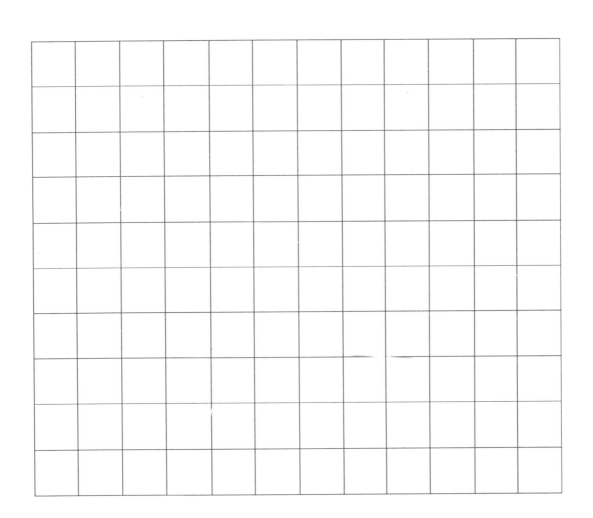

かきましょう

Complete the words using the symbol at the beginning of the line.

さ

	る

	ん	ぽ

	ん

	く	ら

し

	め	て!

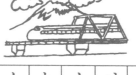
	ん	か	ん	せ	ん

四がつ (四月)

日	月	火	水	木	金	土
1	2	3	4	5	6	7
8	9	10	11	12	13	14
15	16	17	18	19	20	21
22	23	24	25	26	27	28
29	30					

	が	つ

 四

す

お		し

	み	ま	せ	ん

	う	が	く

	い	え	い

せ

	ん		い

	い	と

1000
	ん

	な	か

| そ |

| | ふ |

| | ぼ |

| | ば |

| | の | み | さん |

When you add ﹅ to the symbols in the S line, you make Z sounds. In the first set of boxes, complete the word by using the symbol at the beginning of the line. Then rewrite the word in the second set of boxes. Any symbols that you haven't learned yet have been done for you.

ざ

| お | は | よう |　| ご | | い | ま | す |
↓ ↓
| | は | よ | | | | | ま | |

じ

| し | ち | | → | | ち | |

ず

なまえ:
すずき あきお

| す | | き | | あ | き | お |
↓ ↓
| | | | | | | |

ぜ

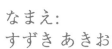

| か | | → | | |

ぞ

| ど | う | | → | ど | | |

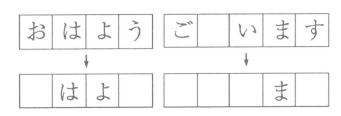  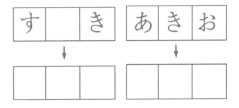  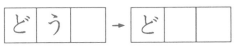

た　た　た　た　た
た　た
ち　ち　ち
ち　ち
つ　つ
つ　つ
て　て
て　て
と　と　ど
と　と

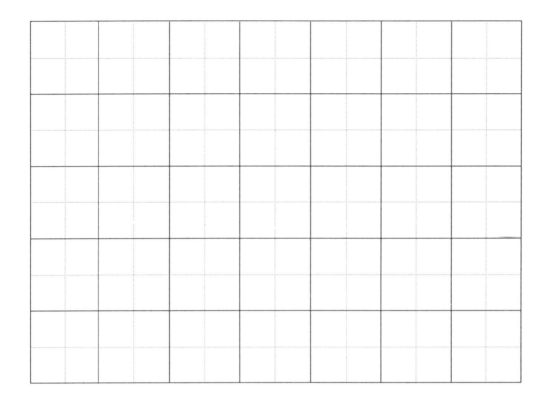

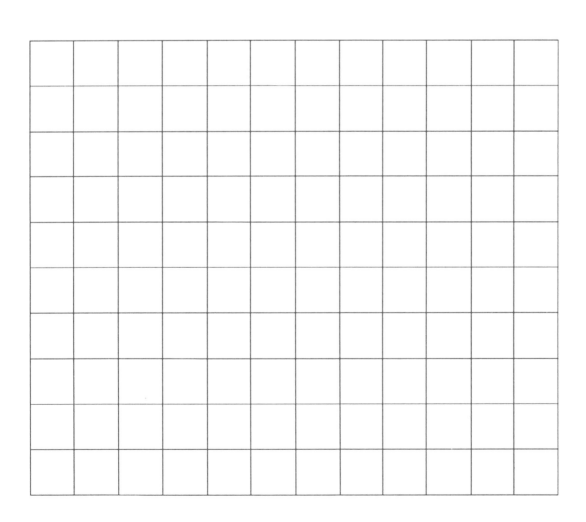

かきましょう

Complete the words using the symbol at the beginning of the line.

た

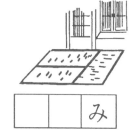

	つ

		み

	い	い	く

	べ	も	の

ち

	ず

	い	さ	い

	か	こ	さ	ん

つ

	き

	る

	く	え

	り

て

…	、

	ん

	が	み

	ん	ぷ	ら

と

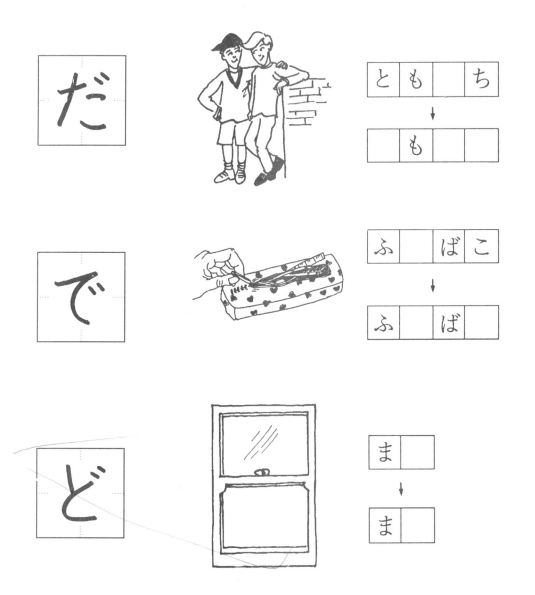

[ ]り

[ ]ら

[ ]けい

[ ]おり

When you add ゛ to the symbols in the T line, you make D sounds. In the first set of boxes, complete the word by using the symbol at the beginning of the line. Then rewrite the word in the second set of boxes. Any symbols that you haven't learned yet have been done for you.

だ

と | も | | ち
↓
| も | |

で

ふ | | ば | こ
↓
ふ | | ば |

ど

ま | |
↓
ま | |

れんしゅう しましょう

A Label these pictures. Write each word in *hiragana*.

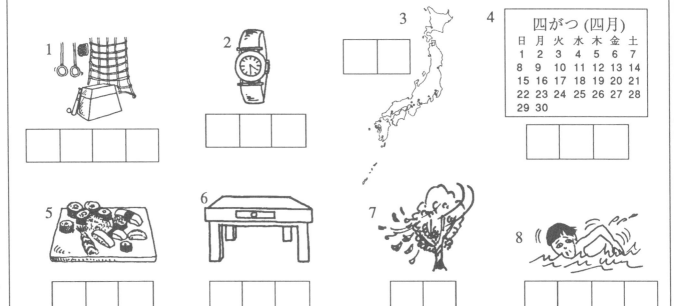

四がつ (四月)

日	月	火	水	木	金	土
1	2	3	4	5	6	7
8	9	10	11	12	13	14
15	16	17	18	19	20	21
22	23	24	25	26	27	28
29	30					

B Highlight the 'odd' ひらがな out in each row.
(Hint: read each line aloud)

1	あ	か	て	さ	た
2	ぎ	さ	じ	ど	が
3	し	ち	さ	そ	せ
4	ど	と	ぞ	そ	こ
5	げ	ぜ	え	お	て

C Many interesting words are made in 日本語 using the ゛ line sounds.
Don't worry about the meaning of these words but try reading them
aloud.

1 ぎくぎく   7 ざくざく
2 ぜんぜん   8 どんどん
3 ぞくぞく   9 ざあざあ
4 ぐずぐず   10 ずんずん
5 がんがん   11 だんだん
6 ごそごそ   12 じとじと

D Let's play しりとり. This is a popular word game in Japan - the last
letter of a word is used as the first letter of the next word. A word
ending in ん finishes the game. Fill in the words to play しりとり.

E You are now able to write seven lines of the ひらがな chart.

	A	I	U	E	O
K					
G					
S					
Z					
T					
D					

(n)	

な	な	な	な	な	
な	な				
に	に	に	に		
に	に				
ぬ	ぬ	ぬ			
ぬ	ぬ				
ね	ね	ね			
ね	ね				
の	の				
の	の				

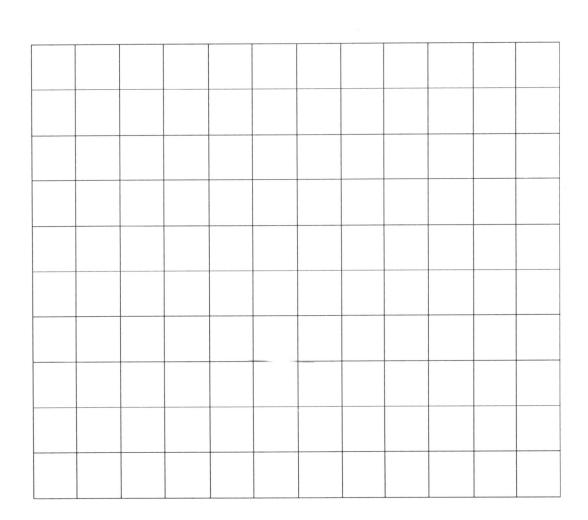

かきましょう

Complete the words using the symbol at the beginning of the line.

な

	つ

お		まえ

	し

	み		さん

に

	ほ	ん	ご

	わ	と	り

	わ

ぬ

い	

こ	い	

ね

	こ

	ず	み

じゃ	ま	た	

	ん	れ	い

の

 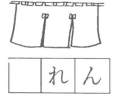 

わ	た	し	

		れ	ん

	み	も	の

	り	ま	き	ず	し

は	は	は	は		
は	は				
ひ	ひ				
ひ	ひ				
ふ	ふ	ふ	ふ	ふ	
ふ	ふ				
へ	へ				
へ	へ				
ほ	ほ	ほ	ほ	ほ	
ほ	ほ				

かきましょう

Complete the words using the symbol at the beginning of the line.

は

  な

  な

  ち

 る

ひ

  つじ

  ざ

  らがな

 と

ふ

  じさん

 ね

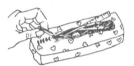 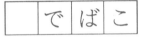 でばこ

 ゆ

へ

 や

  び

  そ

 ええ？

ほ

 ん

 ね

にんご

 し

When you add ﾞ to the symbols in the H line, you make B sounds.

ば
び
ぶ
べ
ぼ

| い | け | | な | → | | | な |

| く | | → | | |

| ざ | | と | ん | → | | | | |

| た | | も | の | → | | | も | |

| | く | → | | |

When you add ○ to the symbols in the H line, you make P sounds.

ぱ
ぴ
ぷ
ぺ
ぽ

| | く | | く | → | | | | |

| え | ん | | つ | → | | | | |

| て | ん | | ら | → | | | ら |

| | こ | | こ | → | | | |

| さ | ん | | → | | | |

れんしゅう しましょう

A Each ひらがな word here is one of a pair, e.g. moon - stars, summer - autumn. Draw a line connecting each pair.

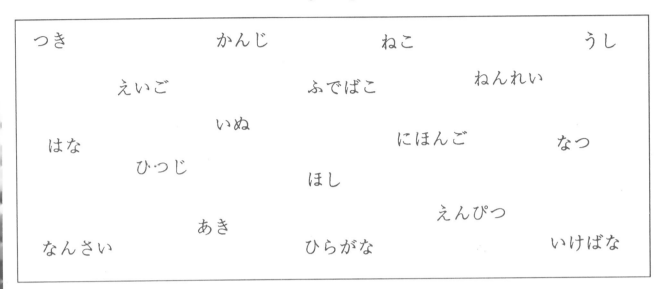

つき　　　　　　かんじ　　　　　　ねこ　　　　　　うし

　　えいご　　　　　　　　ふでばこ　　　　　　　ねんれい

　　　　　　　いぬ

はな　　　　　　　　　　　　　　　　にほんご　　　　　なつ

　　ひつじ　　　　　　　ほし

　　　　　　　　　　　　　　　　　えんぴつ

　　　　あき

なんさい　　　　　　　ひらがな　　　　　　　　いけばな

B Find the ひらがな you need to write the words illustrated.

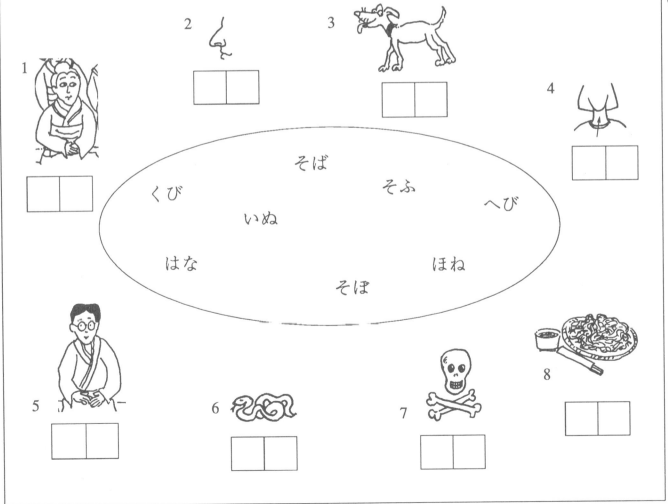

そば

くび　　　　　　　　　　そふ　　　　　　へび

　　　　いぬ

はな　　　　　　　　　　ほね

　　　そぼ

C Practise writing these words both in よこがき (horizontal writing) and たてがき (vertical writing).

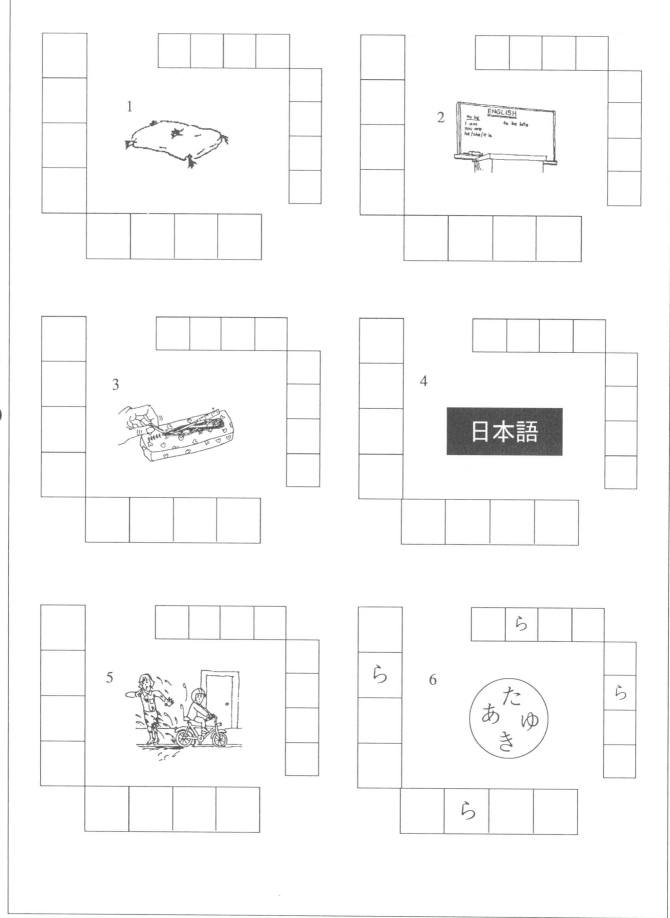

D Read this poem about a hungry little pig.

こぶた　のたのた
おなかが　ぺこぺこ
ぱくぱく　たべた

E You are now able to write eleven lines of the ひらがな chart.

	A	I	U	E	O
K					
G					
S					
Z					
T					
D		(ぢ)	(づ)		
N					
H					
B					
P					

(n)	

ま	ま	ま	ま		
ま	ま				
み	み	み			
み	み				
む	む	む	む		
む	む				
め	め	め			
め	め				
も	も	も	も		
も	も				

や や や や

や や

ゆ ゆ ゆ

ゆ ゆ

よ よ よ

よ よ

かきましょう

Complete the words using the symbol at the beginning of the line.

ま

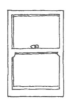
	ど

	ん	が

	つ

	ち

み

	な	さ	ん

	ち	こ	さ	ん

	か	ん

む

	す	こ

	す	め

	ね

	し

め

	が	ね

	い	し

	し	て	！

も

□し□し

□□

□のさし

□みじ

や

□ま

□きそば

□さい

ゆ

□びわ

□び

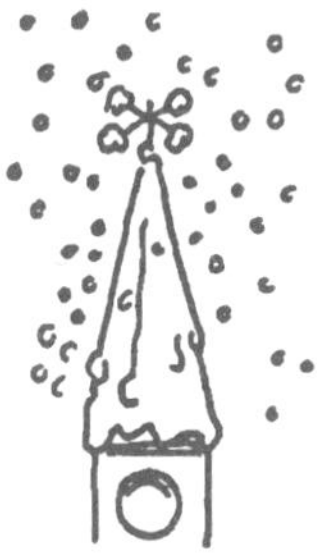

□き

よ

四 □ん

□る

どうぞ...

□ろしく

ら	ら	ら			
ら	ら				
り	り	り			
り	り				
る	る				
る	る				
れ	れ	れ			
れ	れ				
ろ	ろ				
ろ	ろ				

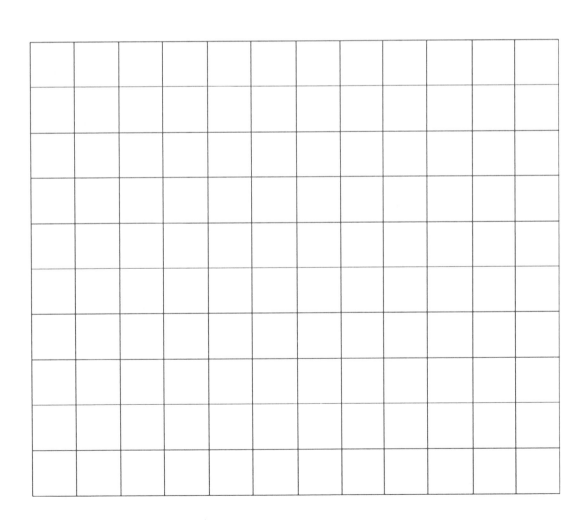

わ　わ　わ

わ　わ

を　を　を　を

を　を

かきましょう

Complete the words using the symbol at the beginning of the line.

ら

	く	だ

さ	く	

さ	

お	て	

り

	ん	ご

	す

お		が	み

こ	と	

る

・・・。

ま	

さ	

く		ま

は	

れ

れきし

zero
□い

□んが

えりこ
ねんれい: 13
ねん□い

ろ

ふろしき

し□

六
□く

おふ□

わ

□たし

□に

□たなべ

ぼくは
わたなべ
です。

でん□

を

えいが
みました。

すいえい
しました。

れんしゅう しましょう

A Label these seasons in ひらがな.

B This is Dorothy. Label the parts of her body indicated.

ひらがな一 ● 五十五

C Highlight the odd word out.

1 わに	りす	らくだ	さる
2 りんご	もも	みかん	やさい
3 えんぴつ	ふでばこ	せんせい	ものさし
4 やま	しろ	かわ	うみ
5 ふろしき	ざぶとん	のれん	ふじさん
6 やきそば	おりがみ	てんぷら	のりまきずし
7 ほんだ	ひたち	すずき	かわさき

D Start reading the snail from the centre, to find out the following information:

a) the word for *snail* in 日本語
b) how old this snail is.

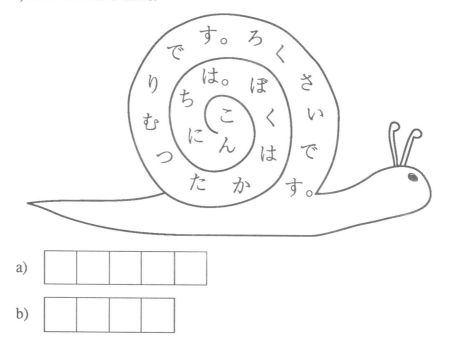

a) ☐☐☐☐☐

b) ☐☐☐☐

E Fill in the missing numbers in ひらがな.

☐☐ , に , ☐☐ , し or ☐☐ , ☐ ,

☐☐ , ☐☐ or なな , はち , ☐ or きゅう

F おめでとう！You are now able to write all of the symbols on the
ひらがな chart.

	A	I	U	E	O
K					
G					
S					
Z					
T					
D		(ぢ)	(づ)		
N					
H					
B					
P					
M					
Y		▒		▒	
R					
W		▒	▒	▒	(o)

(n)	

ひらがな一　●　五十七

ききましょう

A Listen to the teacher giving some instructions in this 日本語 class.
Write the number under the picture as you hear the instruction.

B A roving microphone has picked up people commenting on these
   pictures. As you hear the conversations on the tape, write the number
   under the picture that is being talked about.

C The students are practising classroom commands. Fill in the name of the
   person who is receiving the command.

command	person
sit down!	
listen!	
stand up!	
shut the door!	
look at the board!	
open the window!	

D Terii くん has forgotten to bring his pencil-case to class, so he has to borrow the objects below from other people in the class. Listen to him ask for the various objects and draw a line connecting the object to the person he borrows it from.

E You will hear one word in each group being said. Highlight the word you hear.

1	おおきい	うるさい	おかしい
2	かわいい	きたない	ちいさい
3	おかあさん	おばあさん	はなこさん
4	わたし	ぼく	せんせい
5	えんぴつ	ふでばこ	ものさし

れんしゅうしましょう

A Write in Japanese what would be said in these situations.

1 There's a new student in your class. You want to find out her name.

					?

2 You're trying to concentrate on doing a test, but you are continually distracted by the noise you can hear through the open window.

										。

3 The teacher wants you to look at something on the blackboard.

											。

4 The new kid wants to borrow your pencil.

												。

5 The teacher turns on the tape-recorder and tells everyone to listen!

Teepu									。

B Which of the expressions below would you use in the following situations? More than one comment may be appropriate in each situation.

おおきい ですね。	うるさい ですね。	かわいい ですね。

すごい ですね。	いい おてんき ですね。	きたない ですね。

1 Your friend shows you her brother's very messy bedroom.

_____

2 Your cat has just had five kittens.

_____

3 Your little sister is practising her first violin lesson.

_____

4 Your friend has just received a new set of 72 coloured pencils.

_____

5 The teacher comments on today's really nice weather.

_____

6 You take your little brother to the zoo and he suddenly sees the elephant.

_____

C Look at these expressions taken from the まんが in きもの3 .
   Match each one with the correct frame. Write the number of the
   expression under the frame.

1 いって らっしゃい。   4 ありがとう。
2 どうぞ。   5 みなさん、じゃ またね。
3 おはよう ございます。   6 いって きます。

D まんが
   Read the まんが on pages 二十九 to 三十一 of your textbook, and
   answer these questions.

1 What does Terry ask to borrow from his mother?

   _____

2 Why is the station master surprised?

   _____

3 Which two students give up their seats?

   _____

4 What is Jose's reaction to Terry's behaviour?

   _____

E Pazuru

Fill in the answers to the clues in Japanese horizontally. When you have done this, the mystery sentence will be revealed in the vertical column.

1   The name of this book.
2   I'm Sonomi.
3   It's noisy, isn't it?
4   Please shut it.
5   Look at the blackboard, please.
6   It's cute, isn't it?

7   It's funny, isn't it?
8   Please open it.
9   Please listen.
10 Ms Honda, the teacher.
11 They're small, aren't they?
12 It's dirty, isn't it?

Write the mystery sentence here.

It means

日本に ついて

Read Simone's letter on page 三十六 of the textbook and answer the following questions.

一 Write down four ways in which school life in Japan is similar to yours.

a _____

b _____

c _____

d _____

二 Write down four ways in which school life in Japan is different from yours.

a _____

b _____

c _____

d _____

三 Club activities are a very important part of Japanese school life. Most schools have lots of clubs and students can join academic, sporting and cultural clubs. What clubs does Simone's school have?

_____

_____

_____

四 Look at the address at the top of Simone's letter. If し means *city* and けん means *prefecture*. In what city and prefecture is Simone staying? Try to locate this city on a map of Japan.

city _____

prefecture _____

Can you write out in ひらがな the name of the city and prefecture.

ききましょう

A ゆうこさん wants to fill in her birthday book with her friends'
birthdays. She wants to have it in English. Highlight the correct month
as she asks each of her friends. The first one has been done for you.

1	Peter	April	June	November
2	Sue	January	March	July
3	John	February	October	December
4	Nicole	March	May	September
5	Mario	April	July	September
6	Helen	August	October	November
7	Nick	January	March	February
8	Robyn	December	October	May

B A group of Japanese students is visiting your school. Listen to them
introduce themselves in Japanese. Can you understand how old they
are? Just write down the number.

1 みちこ _____   4 としお _____

2 あきお _____   5 そのみ _____

3 ふみこ _____   6 ただし _____

C Listen to each question and highlight what you are being asked.

1	name	age	address	telephone no.	repeat the question
2	name	age	address	telephone no.	repeat the question
3	name	age	address	telephone no.	repeat the question
4	name	age	address	telephone no.	repeat the question
5	name	age	address	telephone no.	repeat the question
6	name	age	address	telephone no.	repeat the question

D It takes a lot of practice to get used to taking down telephone numbers in
   日本語. See if you can understand these people as they give you their
   numbers in 日本語. Write them down in the spaces below. (0 is *zero*
   or れい in 日本語.)

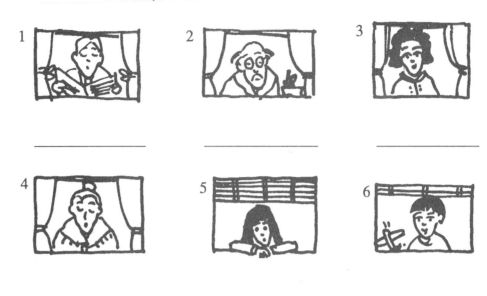

E The lost property office is overflowing. ほんだせんせい has brought
   to class objects belonging to the characters. Listen to her as she passes
   out the items and draw a line linking the person with the correct item.

れんしゅうしましょう

A としおくん is visiting your school for three weeks. He was interviewed for an article in the school newsletter, however the editor (who doesn't understand Japanese) has got the questions and answers mixed up. Draw lines to connect the correct questions and answers.

1 おなまえは?

2 なんさい ですか。

3 たんじょうびは いつ ですか。

4 なにどし ですか。

5 としおくんの じゅうしょは?

6 でんわ ばんごうは なんばん ですか。

1 六がつ です。

2 七八七の 四一三三 です。

3 ぼくは としお です。

4 十四さい です。

5 ひつじどし です。

6 Gratton Streetの 二十四ばん です。

B The きもの characters have entered a contest to guess how many *zerii biinzu* there are in this jar. Below are their entries.

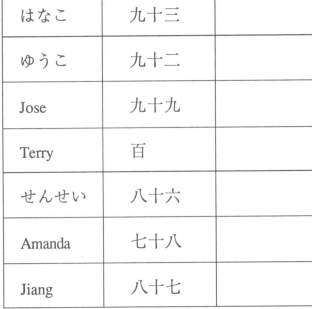

はなこ	九十三	
ゆうこ	九十二	
Jose	九十九	
Terry	百	
せんせい	八十六	
Amanda	七十八	
Jiang	八十七	

1 Write the number that each character guessed in the box.

2 If there are 九十七 *zerii biinzu* in the jar, circle the winner. (The person who is closest wins the prize!)

C See if you can fill in the missing word in each of the conversations
below.

いつ	なん	なんさい	なんばん	なにどし

1 ― ふみこさんは _____ですか。

　 ― 十三さい です。

2 ― ふみこさんの たんじょうびは _____ですか。

　 ― 四がつ です。

3 ― ふみこさんは _____ですか。

　 ― さるどし です。

4 ― でんわ ばんごうは _____ですか。

　 ― 四一二の三四五六 です。

5 ― 日本語で _____ですか。

　 ― えんぴつ です。

D Animalsに ついて
　 Highlight one animal in each group according to the question.

1 Which of these animals wouldn't you have as a pet?

　　いぬ　　うさぎ　　とら　　ねこ

2 Which of these animals was not on Hanako's farm?

　　うし　　うま　　いぬ　　いのしし

3 Which of these animals wouldn't you see in a zoo?

　　ねこ　　さる　　とら　　へび

4 Which of these animals is not in the じゅうにし?

　　かえる　　ねずみ　　ひつじ　　うさぎ

5 Which is the odd one out?

　　ひつじ　　とり　　うし　　うま

E Here is a picture of the すずき *apaato* showing where the people whose telephone number you took down earlier live.

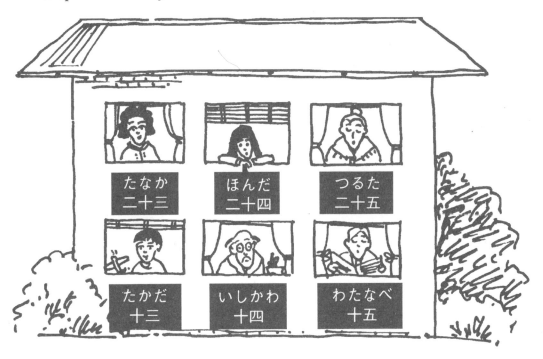

1 Write in the number of each person's apartment on the table below.

apaato	なまえ		でんわ ばんごう
	わたなべ	けいいち	七八六の二三二一
	いしかわ	ただし	六〇六の五九四一
	たなか	きみこ	四七八の九三〇九
	つるた	はなこ	五五四の三八七二
	ほんだ	そのみ	二〇〇の九〇〇〇
	たかだ	たろう	四一二の三六七八

2 Answer these questions about the people who live in the すずき *apaato* in 日本語.

a) Whose telephone number is 606 5941? _____

b) Who lives in apartment number 13? _____

c) What is そのみさん's telephone number? _____

d) Who lives in number 15? _____

e) Whose telephone number is 554 3872? _____

f) Whose telephone number is 478 9309? _____

F まんが

Read these statements about the まんが on pages 四十 to 四十二 of your textbook, and write はい if the statement is correct and いいえ if it is incorrect.

1 Today is Hanako's birthday. _____

2 Hanako likes ice cream. _____

3 The twins' telephone number is 235 8751. _____

4 The twins live at 23 High Street. _____

5 Jose was late because he forgot the twins' telephone number. _____

6 The twins were celebrating their twelfth birthday. _____

G そのみさんは なんさい ですか。

Cross out the numbers in the grid that answer the following questions. The numbers are written horizontally and vertically only. You will need to look at pages 四十四 and 四十五 in your textbook. Two numbers will remain to tell you the answer to the above question.

二	三	四	一	四	八	四	九
四	十	十	十	十	十	四	十
五	五	二	三	二	十	三	二
九	三	五	七	九	一	一	七
三	七	六	十	七	八	三	三
二	十	五	十	二	十	十	十
八	一	四	十	八	一	五	二

1 The telephone numbers of:
   a) Rossi さん
   b) やまださん
   c) たなかさん

2 The ages of:
   a) はなこさん
   b) ゆうこさん
   c) Hose くん
   d) Amanda さん
   e) Terii くん
   f) Jiangu くん
   g) せんせい

3 The house numbers in Yokohama Drive of:
   a) Rossi さん
   b) Pappas さん
   c) Pratt さん
   d) たなかさん

4 The house numbers in Fuji Avenue of:
   a) Hicks さん
   b) やまださん

日本に ついて

一　In Simone's letter on pages 五十 and 五十一 in your textbook she writes about the home of たなかさん. Like you, Simone is pretty good at ひらがな - she wrote about たたみ, いけばな and ふとん. See if you can find pictures or further descriptions of these in your library.

二　Can you find out what these 'house-related' words mean?

1　げんかん

_____

_____

2　とこのま

_____

_____

3　おふろ

_____

_____

4　ふすま

_____

_____

三　Look at the じゅうにし on page 四十五 in your textbook and work out what animal different members of your family are.

_____

_____

_____

_____

_____

— Little や, ゆ, よ

Use the models to practise writing や, ゆ and よ in their smaller forms.

a) よこがき (horizontal writing)

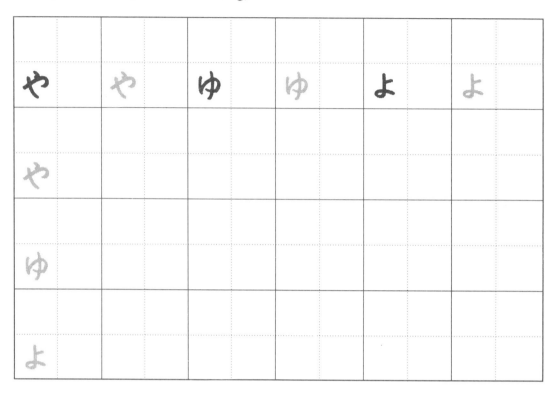

b) たてがき (vertical writing)

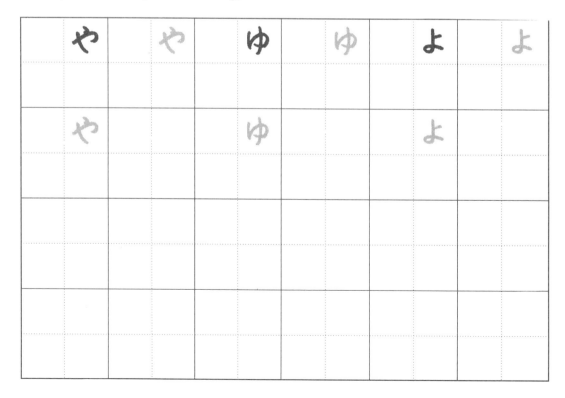

Complete the chart showing little や, ゆ and よ combined with other symbols.

	や	ゆ	よ
き			
ぎ	ぎゃ	ぎゅ	
し			
じ			
ち			
に	にゃ		
ひ		ひゅ	
び		びゅ	
ぴ		ぴゅ	
み	みゃ	みゅ	みよ
り	りゃ		

Practise reading them aloud. Remember they are only one 'beat'.

れんしゅう しましょう

A Practise reading these words.

1 でんしゃ

2 じてんしゃ

3 かしゅ

3-21, Yukinoshita 1-chome, Kamakura-shi, Kanagawa-ken, Japan

4 じゅうしょ

5 おちゃ

6 としょかん

B ひゃく（百）means 100 in Japanese. Write ひゃく in the blank spaces below each price. Then rewrite these labels in the order of the cheapest to most expensive. 円 ＝ ¥.

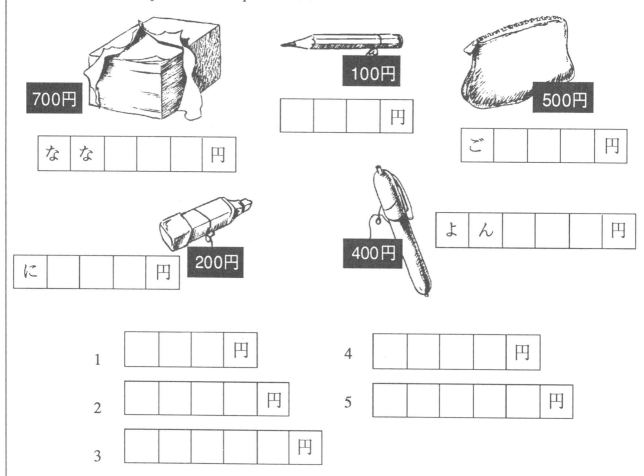

C Here are some interesting sounds which use little や, ゆ and よ.
Practise reading them aloud and then try matching them to their object.
(Remember that often things don't quite sound the same in another language!)

 1   2  3   4

    1 にゃあ にゃあ
    2 びゅん びゅん
    3 ちゅん ちゅん
    4 ぴょん ぴょん

D Label these pictures writing both in よこがき and たてがき.
Take care where you write the smaller symbols.

1
3-21, Yukinoshita 1-chome,
Kamakura-shi, Kanagawa-ken,
Japan

2

3

4

二 Double vowel sounds

A Fill in the bubbles in these まんが from きもの 1 and 2.

B Fill in the blanks.

C In the word たんじょうび, the little よ sound is lengthened in the same way as words like おはよう, おとうさん and ばんごう.

Read these words aloud. They do the same thing. Rewrite them again under the picture.

1 じょうば   2 にんぎょう
3 きょうだい   4 ちょうちん

1 ☐☐☐☐   2 ☐☐☐☐☐

3 ☐☐☐☐☐☐   4 ☐☐☐☐☐

D Look at the たんご list that begins on 百七 *peeji* of your textbook, and write the English meanings of the following words.

1 せんしゅう _____

2 きょう _____

3 だいじょうぶ _____

4 やきゅう _____

5 しゅくだい _____

6 らいしゅう _____

7 じかんひょう _____

E Read aloud the Japanese word for *ambulance*.

きゅうきゅうしゃ

三　Little つ

Little つ is written in the same way as the little や, ゆ and よ. Use the model to practise.

a)　よこがき (horizontal writing)

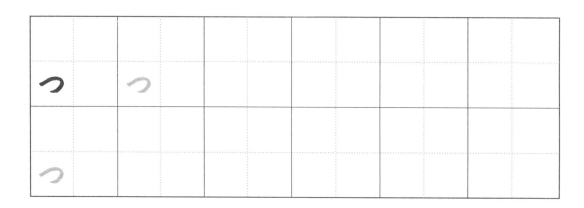

b)　たてがき (vertical writing)

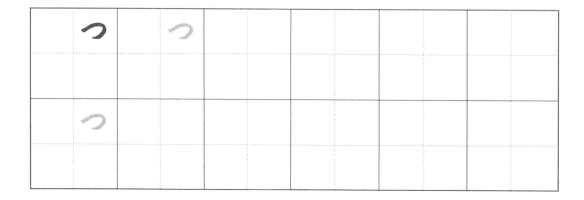

れんしゅう しましょう

A Do you remember the names of the four main islands of Japan?
Write them in the squares.

The capital of Japan is

B What is a...

1 ざっし _____

2 きっぷ _____

3 きって _____

C What are these people being told to do? Write each command in
Japanese.

1

2

3

4

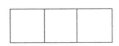

5

6

D Your friend is going to Japan on a short exchange. She hasn't been learning Japanese so she asks you to write down a list of useful expressions that she can use to...

1 say good morning to her friends

| | | | | 。 |

2 say good morning to the teacher

| | | | 、 | | | | | | | | | 。 |

3 ask someone's name

| | | | | ? |

4 thank friends

| | | | | 。 |

5 apologise

| | | | | 。 |

6 comment that it's a nice day

| | | | | | | | | | 。 |

7 agree with someone

| | | | | 。 |

8 borrow a pencil

| | | | | | | | | | | | | | 。 |

9 say that something is cute

| | | | | | | 。 | |

10 wish someone a happy birthday

| (お) | | | | | | | | | | | 。 | |

11 ask how old someone is

| | | | | | | 。 | |

12 say, 'see you later'

| | | | | 。 |

E Complete these words - the first ひらがな has been written in for you.

1

| ふ | | | |

2

| お | | | |

| お | | | |

3
```
3-21, Yukinoshita 1-chome,
Kamakura-shi, Kanagawa-ken,
Japan
```

| じ | ゆ | | | |

4

| せ | | | |

5

| さ | | | | |

F Try saying this tongue-twister in 日本語.

| となりの きゃくは よく かき くう きゃくだ。 |
| *The guest next to me eats lots of persimmons.* |

四　すうじ

一

二

三

四

五

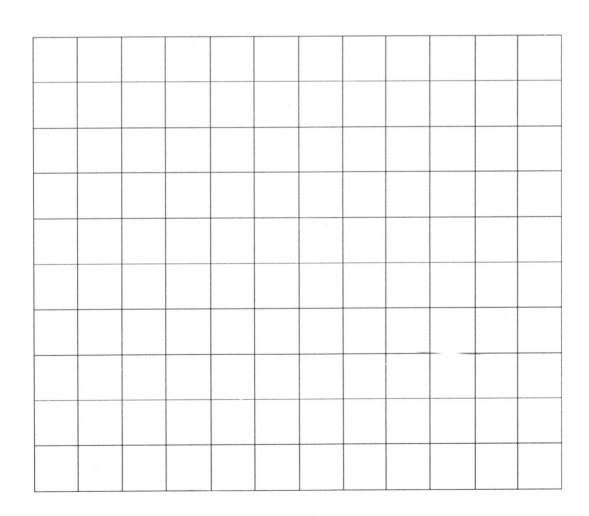

六	六	六	六	六	
六	六				
七	七	七			
七	七				
八	八	八			
八	八				
九	九	九			
九	九				
十	十	十			
十	十				

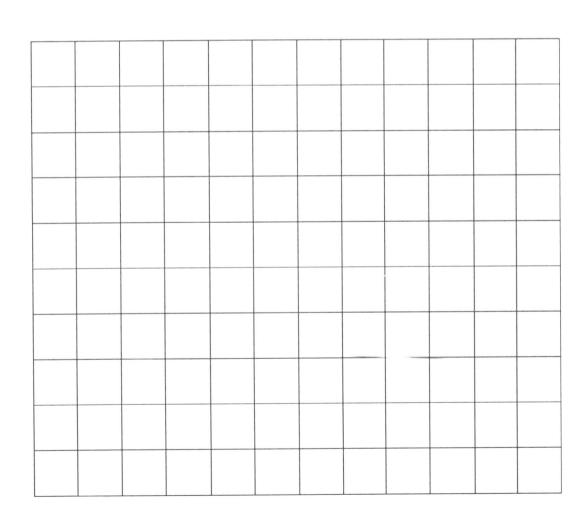

八十五

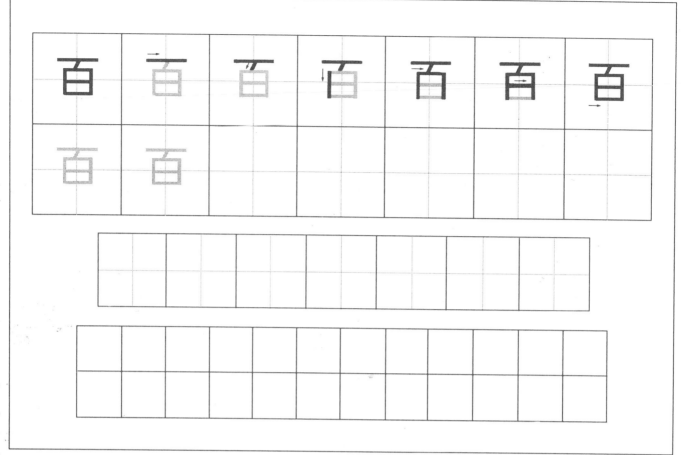

れんしゅう しましょう

A Try solving these すうがく problems using かんじ numbers.

1　二 x 四 =

2　十二 x 三 =

3　二十 x 三 =

4　十八 ÷ 二 =

5　三十 ÷ 六 =

6　四十 ÷ 十 =

7　五十 + 五 =

8　十四 + 三 =

9　六十 + 十 =

10　八十三 − 三 =

11　六十六 − 六 =

12　百 − 九十九 =

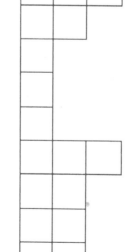

B Using this guide read the above 'problems' aloud. Take it in turns to
   read them with a friend.

x = かける
÷ = わる
+ = たす
− = ひく
=   *ikooru* or は

例: 1 二かける四は八

C Write these かんじ numbers in ひらがな.

1 九 | く | or | | | |

2 十一 | | | | |

3 十 | | |

4 二十 | | | |

5 五十二 | | | | |

6 八十三 | | | | | | | |

7 四十七 | | | | | | | |

8 六十五 | | | | | | |

9 九十一 | | | | | | | | | |

10 七十七 | | | | | | | |

D Complete these series using かんじ numbers.

1 一がつ、＿＿＿＿＿＿ 、＿＿＿＿＿＿ 、四がつ 、＿＿＿＿＿＿ 、
＿＿＿＿＿＿ 、七がつ 、＿＿＿＿＿＿ 、＿＿＿＿＿＿ 、十がつ 、
＿＿＿＿＿＿ 、＿＿＿＿＿＿。

2 十、二十、＿＿＿＿＿＿ 、＿＿＿＿＿＿ 、五十、＿＿＿＿＿＿。

3 九十九、八十八、＿＿＿＿＿＿ 、＿＿＿＿＿＿ 、五十五、＿＿＿＿＿＿。

4 三十五、四十、＿＿＿＿＿＿ 、＿＿＿＿＿＿ 、五十五、＿＿＿＿＿＿ 、
＿＿＿＿＿＿ 、七十。

5 ＿＿＿＿＿＿ 、二十五、四十、＿＿＿＿＿＿ 、七十、＿＿＿＿＿＿ 、百。

6 二十一、三十二、＿＿＿＿＿＿ 、＿＿＿＿＿＿ 、六十五、＿＿＿＿＿＿。

E Fill in the details of these people on their identity cards. Use かんじ
numbers for their age and telephone number.

1
| FUMIKO |
| 13 |
| 426 3791 |

なまえ：
ねんれい：
でんわ ばんごう：

2
| TOSHIO |
| 12 |
| 521 8873 |

なまえ：
ねんれい：
でんわ ばんごう：

3
| SACHIE |
| 11 |
| 673 5454 |

なまえ：
ねんれい：
でんわ ばんごう：

4
| KEIICHI |
| 14 |
| 786 5349 |

なまえ：
ねんれい：
でんわ ばんごう：

き き ま し ょ う

A You will hear some people being asked if they like certain foods. In the boxes under the pictures put ticks or crosses to show:

✓✓	if they really love the food
✓	if they like it
✗	if they don't like it much

1 ☐

2 ☐

3 ☐

4 ☐

5 ☐

6 ☐

7 ☐

8 ☐

B Listen to what is being said in the different classes in a Japanese school. In each case see if you can work out which subjects the teacher and students are doing. Write the appropriate number next to the subject.

たいいく ☐

かがく ☐

えいご ☐

日本語 ☐

おんがく ☐

れきし ☐

すうがく ☐

C Someone is reporting the results of a survey they have done to find out the types of food and drink people like. Use your highlighter pen to indicate:

a) who is being talked about
b) what the person likes

| 1 | はなこさん ゆうこさん ふみこさん | は | おすし おかし おちゃ | が | すき です。 |

| 2 | Teriiくん Jianguくん Hoseくん | は | hotto doggu supagetti hanbaagaa | が | すき です。 |

| 3 | かずこさん さきこさん さちえさん | は | miruku koohi koora | が | すき です。 |

| 4 | わたし ぼく せんせい | は | てんぷら やきそば おかし | が | すきです。 |

| 5 | としおくん あきおくん けいいちくん | は | keeki piza aisukuriimu | が | すき です。 |

| 6 | おとうさん おかあさん おばあさん | は | orenji juusu karee raisu hotto doggu | が | すき です。 |

D Under each subject picture highlight whether the person speaking:

a) likes it or not
b) finds it easy or difficult

1

a
| はい、すき です。 |
| いいえ、あんまり... |

b
| やさしい です。 |
| むずかしい です。 |

2

a
| はい、すき です。 |
| いいえ、あんまり... |

b
| やさしい です。 |
| むずかしい です。 |

3

a
| はい、だいすき です。 |
| いいえ、あんまり... |

b
| やさしい です。 |
| むずかしい です。 |

4

a
| はい、すき です。 |
| いいえ、あんまり... |

b
| やさしい です。 |
| むずかしい です。 |

5

a
| はい、すき です。 |
| いいえ、あんまり... |

b
| やさしい です。 |
| むずかしい です。 |

れんしゅうしましょう

A The きもの characters are thinking about what they like eating and drinking. Write sentences to explain who likes what. Follow the lines to find the information you need.

1 _____ せんせいは orenji juusu が すき です。_____

2 _____

3 _____

4 _____

5 _____

6 _____

7 _____

B Comment on the things below using one of the following expressions. Some expressions may be used more than once.

むずかしい ですね　　やさしい ですね　　おいしい ですね

まずい ですね　　　　おかしい ですね　　うるさい ですね

かわいい ですね

1 _____

2 _____

3 _____

4 _____

5 _____

6 _____

7 _____

8 _____

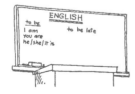

9 _____

10 _____

C Which of the expressions below would you use in the following situations? Use a different expression for each situation.

いただきます　　　ごちそうさま でした
おそく なって すみません　　　いいえ、あんまり...
がんばれ!　　　いいえ　　　おいしい ですね

1 You've just finished eating dinner.

_____

2 You're cheering your friend on at the school sports.

_____

3 You missed the bus and now you have arrived late to class.

_____

4 You're about to start lunch.

_____

5 Your Japanese friend returns your book and thanks you many times.

_____

6 You take a big bite of your friend's ice cream and it tastes really good.

_____

7 You tell your class teacher that you're not very keen on sport when she asks you if you like running. She is looking for a class representative for the school marathon!

_____

D Answer these questions about yourself.

1 おなまえは なん ですか。

_____

2 なんさい ですか。

_____

3 (お)たんじょうびは いつ ですか。

_____

4 なにどし ですか。

_____

5 おんがくは すき ですか。

_____

6 日本語は やさしい ですね。

_____

E Each of the words below is one of a pair. Can you join each pair of
   words? One has been done for you.

いってきます

わたしも

おおきい

やさしい

おとうさん

七がつ

まずい

いただきます

四がつ

ごちそうさま

ぼくも

ちいさい

むずかしい

すわって

いってらっしゃい

たって

おかあさん

おいしい

F まんが
   Read the まんが on pages 五十八 and 五十九 of your textbook and
   answer the following questions in Japanese.

   What did Jose say when he...

   1 arrived late?

   _____

   2 had trouble using chopsticks?

   _____

   3 wished the twins 'Happy Birthday'?

   _____

   4 accepted a piece of cake?

   _____

   5 had finished eating?

   _____

G How would you express the following in Japanese?

1 You want to say how delicious the sushi is.

| | | | | | | | | | | | 。 |

2 You have finished eating your meal at home.

| | | | | | 。 |

3 You ask your friend to sit down.

| | | | | | | | 。 |

4 You ask a new classmate their name.

| | | | | ？ |

5 You invite friends to come in.

| | | | | | | | | | | 。 |

6 You tell your friend to stand up.

| | | | | | | | 。 |

7 Someone asks you if you like pizza, and you answer that you love it.

| | | 、 | | | | | | 。 |

8 You're off to bed.

| | | | | | | | 。 |

9 Someone asks you if you like milk, and you answer that you don't really like it very much.

| | | | 、 | | | | | … |

10 You tell your teacher that you don't understand.

| | | | | | | 。 |

11 You encourage your friend to do their best in the school athletics contest.

| | | | | ！ |

Now, transfer the ひらがな in the ☐ and suggest a situation in which you would use the expression.

| | | | | | | | | | | | 。 |

_____

_____

日本に ついて

やきそばを つくりましょう!

Here is a recipe for やきそば.

ざいりょう

1 pkt egg noodles (cooked)
1/2 cup chopped cabbage
100 gm sliced pork
1 sliced onion
やきそば *soosu* (obtainable from a Japanese supermarket)
or
worcestershire sauce
1 sheet of のり crushed (optional)

つくりかた

1 Fry the onion and pork in some oil.
2 Add the chopped cabbage and lightly fry.
3 Add the noodles and pour over the sauce.
4 Stir until hot and mixed through.
5 Sprinkle のり on top.

おいしい ですよ!

ききましょう

A Listen as some people tell you what they did at the weekend. Write the appropriate かんじ number in the box next to the illustration representing the activity.

B These people are being asked if they did a certain activity last weekend. Highlight what they did.

1 えいがを みました　　まんがを よみました　　かいものを しました
　 おんがくを ききました　しゅくだいを しました　Kooraを のみました

2 えいがを みました　　まんがを よみました　　かいものを しました
　 おんがくを ききました　しゅくだいを しました　Kooraを のみました

3 えいがを みました　　まんがを よみました　　かいものを しました
　 おんがくを ききました　しゅくだいを しました　Kooraを のみました

4 えいがを みました　　まんがを よみました　　かいものを しました
　 おんがくを ききました　しゅくだいを しました　Kooraを のみました

5 えいがを みました　　まんがを よみました　　かいものを しました
　 おんがくを ききました　しゅくだいを しました　Kooraを のみました

6 えいがを みました　　まんがを よみました　　かいものを しました
　 おんがくを ききました　しゅくだいを しました　Kooraを のみました

C たろうくん is reading to the class what he did, ate and drank during
the last week of the holidays. Complete this table to record his activities.

...ようび	...ました	たべました／ のみました
げつようび かようび すいようび もくようび きんようび どようび にちようび	played tennis read comics	 drank coke had やきそば

D いま なんじ ですか。

Listen to what these people replied when asked the above question.
Put the number below the clock showing that time.

E The きもの characters have some tests coming up so last weekend
  they did lots of homework. Draw lines between them and the subject
  in which they did homework.

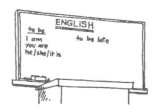

れんしゅうしましょう

A You were doing your 日本語のしゅくだい on a computer when it malfunctioned. Parts of the sentences you were writing were deleted. Fill in the missing words.

1　ほんを _____

2　てんぷらを _____

3　Kooraを _____

4　しゃかいの しゅくだいを _____

5　おんがくを _____

6　けんどうを _____

7　かいものを _____

8　えいがを _____

B Imagine a Japanese tourist stops you in the street and asks,

　— すみません、いま なんじ ですか。

Look at the watches below and write what you would answer.

1 _____ 　 2 _____ 　 3 _____

4 _____ 　 5 _____

C Your little brother has been reading your diary again, so you've decided
   to write it in 日本語.

Saturday:	*played tennis* どようびに tenisu を しました。
Sunday:	*ate hamburgers*
Monday:	*listened to music*
Tuesday:	*watched T.V.*
Wednesday:	*did some shopping*
Thursday:	*did my History homework*
Friday:	*saw a movie*

D This is ふみこさん's homework schedule from last week. Answer
   the questions about ふみこ in complete Japanese sentences.

しゅくだい		
げつようび:	しゃかい	かがく
かようび:	すうがく	日本語
すいようび:	れきし	
もくようび:	すうがく	おんがく
きんようび:	えいご	

1 げつようびに かがくの しゅくだいを しましたか。

   _____

2 もくようびに すうがくの しゅくだいを しましたか。

   _____

3 すいようびに なにを しましたか。

   _____

4 きんようびに おんがくの しゅくだいを しましたか。

   _____

5 かようびに えいごの しゅくだいを しましたか。

   _____

E **まんが**
   Read the まんが on pages 六十九 to 七十一 of your textbook.
   Amanda's weekend seemed pretty harmless, didn't it?

   Amanda さんは uiikuendoに なにを しましたか。

   _____

   _____

   _____

   _____

   _____

   What did her friends say about what she did?

   _____

F   Fill in this grid with your own timetable in 日本語.

じかんひょう

G Someone hid a microphone in the locker room on Monday morning and recorded this conversation about homework.

Helen:	Robinさん、日本語の しゅくだいを しましたか。
Robin:	ええ、しました。 Herenさんは?
Helen:	ええ、わたしも 日本語の しゅくだいを しました。
	Piitaaくん、日本語のしゅくだいを しましたか。
Peter:	いいえ、でも すうがくの しゅくだいを しました。
Mario:	Robaatoくん、uiikuendoに しゅくだいを しましたか。
Robert:	ええ、かがくの しゅくだいを しました。 Marioくんは?
Mario:	ぼくは えいごの しゅくだいを しました。
Helen:	Suuさん、えいごの しゅくだいを しましたか。
Sue:	いいえ、でも かいものを しました。
Everyone:	えっ?

With your highlighter pen record who has done what homework.

1 Robin 日本語 すうがく えいご れきし かがく no homework done

2 Helen 日本語 すうがく えいご れきし かがく no homework done

3 Peter 日本語 すうがく えいご れきし かがく no homework done

4 Robert 日本語 すうがく えいご れきし かがく no homework done

5 Mario 日本語 すうがく えいご れきし かがく no homework done

6 Sue 日本語 すうがく えいご れきし かがく no homework done

Em.
4 days 2 go.

H たこは なにを しましたか。 Write these sentences in Japanese along the octopus' tentacles and the mystery sentence will reveal what the たこ did last night.

1 What time is it?
2 I listened to music.
3 We watched a movie.
4 We did some shopping.
5 I read a book.
6 She drank tea.
7 He did karate.
8 We ate sweets.
9 I did homework.

What did the たこ do last night? Rewrite the symbols in the tentacles marked ○.

ききましょう

A These students of 日本語 have to tell the class where they went yesterday and what they did there. For each student, highlight what he or she did at a particular place.

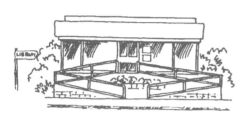

1 read a book
   did homework

2 had Japanese food
   ate fast food

3 went for a swim
   had an ice cream

4 did shopping
   saw a film

5 listened to tapes
   watched T.V.

B Mario is talking about a photo of his family.
  For each person he points out:

  • who they are
  • their age
  • what they like

  Highlight the correct alternative for each person.

1	おじいさん / おばあさん	76 / 67	keeki / koora
2	おとうさん / おかあさん	45 / 42	えいが / おんがく
3	おにいさん / おねえさん	17 / 19	supootsu / かいもの
4	おとうとさん / いもうとさん	10 / 11	tenisu / すいえい

C These people are being asked about their weekend. Write the appropriate
   number under each drawing.

D Now listen to the interviews again and highlight the word that best
   describes what they did.

1 おいしかった   つまらなかった   たのしかった   よかった   あつかった
2 おいしかった   つまらなかった   たのしかった   よかった   あつかった
3 おいしかった   つまらなかった   たのしかった   よかった   あつかった
4 おいしかった   つまらなかった   たのしかった   よかった   あつかった
5 おいしかった   つまらなかった   たのしかった   よかった   あつかった
6 おいしかった   つまらなかった   たのしかった   よかった   あつかった

A Look at this person's diary for last week. For each day write where you think they went. The first has been done for you.

Monday	Tuesday	Wednesday	Thursday	Friday	Saturday	Sunday
took the dog for a walk	*ate Japanese food*	*watched T.V. with a friend*	*borrowed some books*	*bought a new tape*	*went swimming*	*went sailing* (it was really hot all weekend)

1 こうえんに いきました。

2 _____

3 _____

4 _____

5 _____

6 _____

7 _____

B Complete this table.

is...	was...
むずかしい	
	うるさかった
	おおきかった
ちいさい	
いい	
	おいしかった
まずい	
	きたなかった
つまらない	
やさしい	

C どこに いきましたか。なにを しましたか。
　どう でしたか。

Under each of these pictures write in 日本語 where each
person went at the weekend and what they did.
Write what comment they may have made.

1

_____

_____

_____

2

_____

_____

_____

3

_____

_____

_____

4

_____

_____

_____

5

_____

_____

_____

6

_____

_____

_____

D どう でしたか。

You are telling some friends about your recent family holiday at the beach. Your little sister keeps on butting in with comments about what it was like. What does she say? Choose one of the following expressions for each situation.

まずかったですよ　　あつかったですよ

たのしかったですよ　　おいしかったですよ

おかしかったですよ　　つまらなかったですよ

1　On the first day it rained all day.

_____

2　The next day you went to the beach and got sunburned.

_____

3　You ate watermelon and ice cream on the beach.

_____

4　Your dog was thirsty and drank your coke. Everyone laughed.

_____

5　Someone knocked over the bottle of coke onto the picnic lunch, so you had to eat soggy sandwiches.

_____

6　You had a really great holiday!

_____

E　Read these statements about the まんが on pages 八十一 to 八十三 of your textbook, and write はい if the statement is correct and いいえ if it is incorrect.

1　せんしゅうの どようび は とても あつかった です。_____

2　みんなは うみに いきました。_____

3　Terii くんの puuru は あたらしい です。_____

4　みんなは Terii くんの うちに いきました。_____

5　Terii くんの いもうとさんの puuru は おおきいです。_____

6　みんなは すいえいを しました。_____

F はなこさんと ゆうこさんの かぞく

Complete the following sentences about the twins' family.

1 おじいさんの なまえは ＿＿＿＿＿＿＿＿＿＿＿＿＿です。

2 おばあさんの なまえは ＿＿＿＿＿＿＿＿＿＿＿＿＿です。

3 あきらくんは はなこさんと ゆうこさんの

＿＿＿＿＿＿＿＿＿＿＿＿＿です。

4 としおくんは はなこさんと ゆうこさんの

＿＿＿＿＿＿＿＿＿＿＿＿＿です。

5 おかあさんは ＿＿＿＿＿＿＿＿＿＿＿＿＿ さい です。

なまえは ＿＿＿＿＿＿＿＿＿＿＿です。

6 ＿＿＿＿＿＿＿＿＿＿＿＿ は 四十五さい です。

なまえは ＿＿＿＿＿＿＿＿＿＿＿です。

G You have to talk about a photograph of your family in your Japanese class. You were in a hurry this morning and of course forgot to bring yours. Your friend in another class lends you his. This is a little embarrassing as you don't know anything about the family so you have to make it all up and bluff your way through. (You really hope that せんせい doesn't ask you too many questions!)
Write what you will say about each family member (including yourself!). You could talk about their names, ages, favourite things, where they've been recently etc.

H Complete the sentences below using the appropriate instruction word
   from the following list.

やめて   みて   きて   あがって

はいって   まって   きいて

   1 Teepuを＿＿＿＿＿＿くだ さい。

   2 どうぞ＿＿＿＿＿＿くだ さい。

   3 Puuruに＿＿＿＿＿＿くだ さい。

   4 ちょっと ＿＿＿＿＿＿くだ さい。

   5 あぶない ですよ。 ＿＿＿＿＿＿!

   6 Paatiiに＿＿＿＿＿＿くだ さい。

   7 こくばんを ＿＿＿＿＿＿くだ さい。

I Pazuru
   Amanda was very busy last week. Below is a list of the different places
   she went to and things she did. Find these words in the grid. They are
   written both よこ (horizontally) and たて (vertically). Four ひらがな
   will remain to tell you what she thought about her busy week.

よ	ま	ち	か	ら	て	か
す	こ	と	し	ょ	か	ん
い	う	え	が	っ	こ	う
え	え	い	か	い	も	の
い	ん	が	っ	に	わ	た
と	も	だ	ち	の	う	ち

まち   かいもの   こうえん   えいが
からて   としょかん   にわ
がっこう   すいえい   ともだち の うち

☐☐☐☐ です。

It was ＿＿＿＿＿＿＿＿.

日本 に ついて

日本

1 Below is a jumbled list of Japanese place names (islands and cities).
   Highlight in different colours,

    a) the names of the main islands that make up Japan
    b) the names of cities

    さっぽろ
    ひろしま
    ほんしゅう
    きょうと
    おおさか
    きゅうしゅう
    しこく
    ながさき
    ほっかいどう
    とうきょう
    おきなわ
    なら

2 Without looking at your text, try and
   label the map of 日本 with the islands
   and cities listed above, in ひらがな.

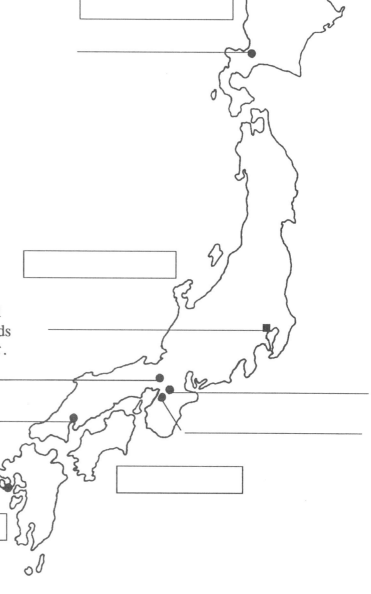

ききましょう

A Listen carefully to these conversations and draw a line between each person's destination and the mode of transport.

ひろしま

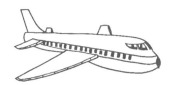

B You will hear people being asked about their plans for today and tomorrow. Highlight for each person who they are planning to go out with.

1 Herenさん:	おばあさん	おじいさん	おとうと
2 Robaatoくん:	Herenさん	Suuさん	Robinさん
3 Robinさん:	ともだち	ともこさん	Tomuくん
4 Marioくん:	いぬ	あに	あね
5 Suuさん:	けいこさん	けいいちくん	けんじくん

C Listen to these mini conversations and decide what is being talked about. Highlight your choice.

1 suggesting going somewhere   finding out plans   arranging a time   suggesting how to get somewhere

2 suggesting going somewhere   finding out plans   arranging a time   suggesting how to get somewhere

3 suggesting going somewhere   finding out plans   arranging a time   suggesting how to get somewhere

4 suggesting going somewhere   finding out plans   arranging a time   suggesting how to get somewhere

5 suggesting going somewhere   finding out plans   arranging a time   suggesting how to get somewhere

6 suggesting going somewhere   finding out plans   arranging a time   suggesting how to get somewhere

D Robaato くん and Robin さん are best friends and at the holiday camp they plan their programme of activities so that they can do everything together. Listen to their conversation and circle on the programme below what they will do.

じかん		
9.00		
10.30		
12.00		
1.30		
3.00		
4.30		
6.00		
7.30		

れんしゅうしましょう

A The きもの characters are getting ready for なつやすみ!

   a) Follow the lines to find out where each person is going and write
      it below.

   b) Write another sentence saying what they might do at that place.

1 _____

  _____

2 _____

  _____

3 _____

  _____

4 _____

  _____

5 _____

  _____

6 _____

  _____

B Since Simone has been in Japan, she has been shopping with the Tanaka's, gone to the baseball and watched Scott hit a home run, and been on a school trip. Following are some excerpts from the diary she has been keeping in 日本語. Fill in the gaps using one of the following.

と	で	に	を

1 わたしは たなかさんの かぞく_____かいもの _____

   いきました。でんしゃ _____ いきました。

2 せんしゅうの どようび _____ やきゅうの geemu _____

   みました。

3 しんかんせん_____ きょうと _____ いきました。

4 五じはん _____ とうきょうえき _____ いきました。

5 六じ_____せんせい _____あいました。

6 ふじさん _____ みました。

7 ともだち _____ なら _____ いきました。

   とても たのしかった です。

C A Japanese student is staying at your place for a week. Suggest what the situation might be if your new friend says the following expressions.

1 いいえ、わかりません。

   _____

2 ゆっくり いって ください。

   _____

3 じゅうしょって、えいごで なん ですか。

   _____

4 いもうとさんの おなまえは?

   _____

5 えっ、なに?

   _____

6 おそく なって すみません。

   _____

7 えいごは むずかしい ですね。

_____

8 ええ、だいすき です。

_____

9 ちょっと まって...

_____

10 いただきます。

_____

D Read these statements about the まんが on pages 九十三 to 九十六 of your textbook and highlight the correct alternative.

1 なつやすみは　　らいしゅう　　から です。
　　　　　　　　　あした

2 はなこさんと ゆうこさんは　　かぞく　　と 日本に いきます。
　　　　　　　　　　　　　　　ともだち

3 らいしゅうの　　きんようび　に 日本に いきます。
　　　　　　　　　かようび

4 はなこさんと ゆうこさんは　　きょうと　　に いきます。
　　　　　　　　　　　　　　　とうきょう

5 ひこうきは　　四じ　　に でます。
　　　　　　　七じ

6 みんなは　　でんしゃ　で くうこうに いきました。
　　　　　　　basu

7 はなこさんと ゆうこさんは　　ひこうき　で 日本に いきます。
　　　　　　　　　　　　　　　しんかんせん

E Friends of your parents are going to spend a few days in Japan. They have organised some of their itinerary and would like you, as a student of 日本語, to write it in 日本語 so they can send it to their Japanese friends. It seems that they will be able to meet these friends on the Friday and so have included that suggestion in their itinerary. Write it out below.

Sunday

· go to the Ginza by train _____

· do some shopping _____

· eat *tenpura* _____

Monday

· go to Kyoto on the super express train _____

· see Mt Fuji _____

Tuesday

· go to the Ryoanji Temple _____

· see the Golden Pavilion _____

· have *sukiyaki* _____

Wednesday

· go to Nara by bus _____

· see the big Buddha (だいぶつ) _____

Thursday

· go for a walk _____

· meet friends at 7.00 _____

· go to a restaurant _____

· eat *sushi* with friends _____

Friday

Let's meet at 10.00? _____

Saturday

· go to the airport by bus at 4.00 _____

· plane leaves at 8.30 _____

F A Japanese visitor, すずきさん, is coming to speak to your class. As you are on the School Magazine Committee, you have been asked to interview the visitor. You might like to know her age, what she enjoys (food, sports etc.), where she's been and what she's done since being in your country, and where she is going next. You will need to have at least six questions prepared. Don't forget to get her address so you can send her a copy of your article. Write your questions below.

_____

_____

_____

_____

_____

_____

_____

_____

Now, interview one of your classmates as if he or she is すずきさん and write an article to include in the school magazine.

_____

_____

_____

_____

_____

_____

_____

_____

G Plan an ideal weekend for yourself (no homework or housework). What
   will you do? Where will you go? Who with?

どようび		

にちようび		

H Pazuru

Write in the first vertical column how you would ask someone their plans for tomorrow. (What are you going to do tomorrow?)

```
1 [  ][  ][  ]
2 [  ][  ][  ][  ][  ]
3 [  ][  ][  ][  ][  ]
4 [  ][  ]
5 [  ][  ][  ][  ]
を
6 [  ][  ][  ][  ][  ]
7 [  ]
8 [  ][  ][  ]
9 [  ][  ][  ][  ]
```

You now have a hint to complete each line of the puzzle. Write the missing word from the sentences below into the appropriate line.

1 きょうは げつようび です。　＿＿＿＿＿＿ は かようび です。

2 きのう すうがくの ＿＿＿＿＿＿ を しました。 むずかしかった です。

3 きょうは ぼくの ＿＿＿＿＿＿ です。＿＿＿＿＿＿ おめでとう!
　(hint: it's the same word)

4 Uiikuendoに ＿＿＿＿＿＿ を しますか。 うみに いきますか。

5 きょうは どようび です。 あしたは ＿＿＿＿＿＿です。 Uiikuendo です。

6 はなこさんと ゆうこさんは たぶん きょうとに ＿＿＿＿＿＿ で いきます。

7 かいものを します。＿＿＿＿＿＿ に いきます。

8 - あつい ですね。＿＿＿＿＿＿ に いきましょうか。
　- ええ、うみに いきましょう。

9 きのう ぎんざに いきました。 ＿＿＿＿＿＿を しました。
　たのしかった です。

日本に ついて

How much do you know about famous places and things in Japan? Match the 日本語 in the left-hand column with the appropriate explanation in the right-hand column. You might have to refer to Simone's letters in きもの 7 and 8.

1	しんかんせん	the first capital of Japan
2	とうきょう	all that glitters is gold at this temple
3	とうきょう tawaa	a temple with a really famous rock garden
4	きょうと	Tokyo's Eiffel Tower
5	きんかくじ	a very fast way to move around
6	りょうあんじ	it's a very high volcano
7	だいぶつでん	the second capital of Japan
8	なら	a famous place to do some shopping
9	ぎんざ	wow! what a big Buddha!
10	ふじさん	the third capital of Japan